— THE PET SITTER —

The Pet Sitter

Tana Reiff

Grass Roots Press

The Pet Sitter
© Tana Reiff 2020
www.grassrootsbooks.net

Acknowledgements

Grass Roots Press acknowledges the financial support of the Government of Canada for our publishing activities.

Canadä

Produced with the assistance of the Government of Alberta through the Alberta Media Fund.

Alberta

Design: Lara Minja, Lime Design Inc.

Library and Archives Canada Cataloguing in Publication

Title: The pet sitter / Tana Reiff.
Other titles: Other people's pets
Names: Reiff, Tana, author.
Series: Reiff, Tana. Working for myself.
Description: Series statement: Working for myself | Originally published under title: Other people's pets. Belmont, CA : Lake Education, ©1994.
Identifiers: Canadiana 20200241672 | ISBN 9781771533478 (softcover)
Subjects: LCSH: Readers for new literates.
Classification: LCC PE1126.N43 R444585 2020 | DDC 428.6/2—dc23

1

A Love for Animals

Rocky was an old brown mutt with the kindest dog heart in the world. Now he lay dying. Rocky had been Ginny's best boy since she was a little girl. She was grown up now, but still living with her mom and two brothers.

She just sat on the grass beside Rocky, petting him.

She remembered the day she found Rocky. He was in a box by the side of the road. A sign on the box said: FREE PUPPY. Ginny took him home. She loved him right away.

"What's that little rag?" her mom said when she saw the dirty little puppy.

"Oh, please, can we keep him?" Ginny begged her mom.

"Give him a bath," her mom said. "We'll decide after he's cleaned up."

Ginny got a bucket and filled it with water. She rubbed soap all over the puppy. He stood still and let Ginny wash him. Then he jumped around and shook himself. Ginny dried him with a towel. The puppy looked like a soft ball of fur.

"Please, Mom?" she asked again. The puppy went over to Ginny's mom. He looked right into her eyes. His eyes melted her heart.

"How can I say no?" her mom said with a laugh.

All the time Ginny was growing up, Rocky was her buddy. He grew much too large for a bucket bath, but he always had a baby face. He seemed almost like a brother to Ginny, even though she had two real brothers. Rocky loved her—no matter what.

Now, Rocky was old and very sick. Ginny knew he couldn't last much longer. She stroked his fur. She fed him out of her hand. The old boy could hardly lift his head.

Then Rocky closed his eyes for the last time. He was gone.

Ginny cried and cried, and then she dug a grave in the backyard. After burying Rocky, she marked it with a stone. She painted ROCKY on it in big letters.

"Why don't you get another dog?" Ginny's mom asked her.

"There can never be another Rocky," Ginny said.

Then one day Ginny's friend Eva called. Eva had her own place, where she lived alone. "I'm going away for a week," Eva said. "I don't want to leave my dog in a kennel. She would much rather stay home. Could you come by every day and feed her?"

Ginny wasn't sure she was ready to take care of someone else's dog. But she understood how Eva felt.

She would have hated to leave Rocky in a kennel. So she said, "OK."

"Stop over for the key and stay a while," said Eva. "That way, Poppy can get to know you. Of course, I want to pay you for helping out."

"You don't have to pay me," Ginny told her friend.

"Come on!" Eva said. "I'd pay plenty to board her at a kennel. Don't put up a fight. Just get over here."

Ginny put on her coat and drove over to Eva's house.

Poppy was a little black furry thing, not at all like Rocky. When Ginny walked in, the dog sniffed her up and down. She knew Ginny right away. She just kept on sniffing anyway.

"Poppy looks really pretty," said Ginny, petting the soft fur.

"I just finished clipping her today," said Eva. "I love grooming my Poppy!"

The dog sniffed Ginny's hand.

"And you painted her nails pink, just like yours!" said Ginny.

"We are almost like sisters!" said Eva.

Then Eva showed Ginny where she kept the dog food. She showed how much to feed Poppy. She gave Ginny a leash so she could walk Poppy around the neighborhood.

Then Ginny noticed Eva's plants. "Do you want me to water your plants while you're away?" Ginny asked. "I might as well."

"That would be great!" said Eva. "I won't have a thing to worry about. And will you be sure to give my baby some TLC every day?"

Ginny picked up Poppy and rubbed her head. "That goes without saying," she said. "Tender loving care is part of the deal!"

"You really *do* love animals, don't you?" Eva asked.

"I do," said Ginny. "I thought I only loved Rocky. But maybe I loved Rocky so much because I love all animals so much."

"You know, there are people who do pet sitting for a living," said Eva.

"Really? They go into people's homes to take care of their pets?"

"Oh, yeah," said Eva. "Lots of people have pets. And lots of people worry when they go away and can't take their pet along. They want their pets to be happy and healthy at home when they're not with them."

Ginny didn't say anything. She was thinking to herself.

"Pet sitting would be good work for you," said Eva. "You're cut out for it. That's why I asked you to take care of Poppy."

"I already have a job," Ginny said. "I'd rather not work nights, but it's a job."

"That crummy job? Heck, you could pet sit during the day and still keep your job," Eva said.

Eva gave Ginny a door key. "Here," she said. "Guard this key with your life. I hope everything goes fine with my baby. I know she's in good hands."

"Don't worry," said Ginny. "And I'll think about what you said. If looking after Poppy goes well, maybe one thing will lead to another."

"We'll see, won't we?" Eva said with a laugh.

Ginny stopped by Eva's place the next day and the day after that. The third day she went twice. She was getting to like these little visits. Pet sitting didn't seem like work at all.

2

Something to Work On

Eva's dog was a little jumpy. She was no good at playing "stick." All she wanted to do was run and jump like a rabbit. She was very different from Rocky.

But Ginny couldn't help but like this dog. She wondered if she could learn to like cats, too. She had always thought of herself as a dog person.

Her chance came after Eva came home. "You did a great job with Poppy," Eva told Ginny. "My aunt is leaving town soon. She has a cat. She wants a pet sitter. Can I give her your number?"

"I guess so," Ginny said. "I don't know much about cats, though."

"I'll tell you the main difference," said Eva. "A dog likes to please people. A cat has a mind of its own. And most cats have litter boxes. If you ask me, those things are no fun at all to clean out. But then neither are a dog's ears, and I do that."

Eva always made Ginny laugh. "Cleaning a litter box wouldn't be my favorite job, either," she said.

So she made plans to take care of Eva's aunt's cat.

But before the time came, Ginny looked around online and found four pet sitters nearby. She called them all, which took some guts.

For the first one, Ginny pretended to be a customer. She knew it was sneaky. But she wanted to find out how much pet sitters charge for their work.

The second pet sitter said she didn't care to share the secrets of her successful business. But she said there was plenty of pet-sitting work around. "Just don't take my clients!" she added.

The third pet sitter gave Ginny some tips on buying insurance. He said that two types were important to have: liability insurance and bonding. Ginny asked what the difference was and he explained.

Suppose something bad happened to a home when the pet sitter was there. Suppose something happened to the animal. Suppose the pet sitter lost the door key and new locks had to be put in. Suppose the pet owner sued the pet sitter. Even if the pet sitter did nothing wrong, getting sued could cost a lot of money. It could put the sitter out of business. Yes, the man told Ginny, in case anything like that happened, she needed liability insurance.

A pet sitter also needed to be bonded, the man explained. Some people might worry that a pet sitter would steal things. With bonding, they could rest easy. If it turned out you weren't honest, the bonding company would pay for anything that went missing. Then the pet sitter would have to pay back the bonding company. Yes, the man told Ginny, a pet sitter needed to be bonded.

"I'll look into liability insurance and bonding," Ginny said.

She couldn't thank the man enough for his advice.

She got more tips from the last person on the list. This young woman had started her own pet-sitting business in high school. Now she had five people working for her. She always had someone to fill in when needed. The workers did most of the pet sitting. The owner spent most of her time running the business.

This woman told Ginny to keep track of every mile she drove. She told her to write down all the money she spent on the business. She also said that most of her work came by word of mouth. One person would tell another, and so on, and so on. She gave Ginny ideas for how to start that word of mouth.

The next day Ginny got out of bed a little early. She ate breakfast faster than usual. She skipped checking her phone. She got in her car and drove to a pet shop.

"My name is Ginny Carr," she told the friendly man behind the counter. "I was wondering—does anyone ever ask you about pet sitting?"

"As a matter of fact, they do," said the man.

"Well, I'm looking for pet-sitting work," said Ginny. "I have another job, but it starts at 5:00 p.m. I can take care of pets during the day."

"You're welcome to put up a little sign or your business card." He pointed to the bulletin board next to the door.

"I don't have a business card," Ginny said. "For now, I'll make a little sign."

The man gave Ginny a piece of paper and a pen.

She wrote PET SITTING at the top of the paper. Under that she wrote: "Going away? Leave your pet in good hands. Call Ginny Carr!" She wrote her name and phone number sideways across the bottom of the paper ten times. Then she tore the paper between each spot. People could tear off her name and number to take along with them.

"Thanks so much," Ginny told the man at the pet store.

"You're quite welcome," he said. "I hope you get some business out of it!"

Next, Ginny went to an animal doctor's office. They let her put up a sign, too. But the vet's helper said, "Really, it would be better if we could hand out your business card."

"I don't have a business card," Ginny said for the second time that day. "I guess I should take care of that."

When Ginny got home she ordered 100 business cards online. She picked a card with pictures of dogs and cats and filled in her contact information.

Then she got ready to go to work. As she closed the door behind her, a picture of Rocky popped into her head. Tears came to her eyes. It was the first time she had thought of her dog all day.

3

First Real Job

The phone's screen said "J Hobbs." Ginny didn't know anyone named Hobbs, but she answered anyway.

J Hobbs was Jeanne Hobbs. "I got your number at the vet's office," she told Ginny. "I was taking my pup for a check-up before I go away."

Then she started asking a lot of questions. After all, she just *loved* her dog. She did not want to leave her darling girl with just anyone for two weeks.

"How long have you been in the pet-sitting business?" Jeanne Hobbs asked.

"To tell the truth, I'm just getting started. But I took good care of my own dog for 14 years. And I've taken care of two people's pets since my Rocky died."

"How do I know I can count on you?" Jeanne asked.

"I love animals," said Ginny. "I'll treat your pet like my own. I have a full-time job, and I never miss work. I am always on time. When I say I will be somewhere, I will be there."

"But how do I know I can really trust you? Not only with Muffy, but in my home."

"I'm getting insurance," said Ginny. "By later today, I will be insured and bonded."

Then Ginny had an idea. "Tell you what. I'll give you my friend Eva's number. I took care of her dog last month. She can tell you what she thinks of my work."

Jeanne Hobbs hung up. She called back in five minutes. "Your friend gives you high marks, all right. Why don't you come over and meet my Muffy?"

Muffy. Ginny hated that name. It made her think of a spoiled mama's baby. But this might be a good test. If she could take care of a dog named Muffy, she could take care of anything. "Sure, just give me your address. I can come by after lunch."

Ginny felt nervous as soon as she walked into Jeanne's living room. She could tell right away the woman would be a fussy customer. Everything was set up like a show home. Not a speck of dust anywhere. Everything neat and tidy. Furniture and rugs that must have cost a lot of money. Ginny took off her shoes to make sure she wouldn't track in any dirt.

And there was Muffy: a little white dog wearing a tiny red jacket! The little dog jumped up and put her paws all over Ginny. Jeanne said nothing—just picked her up and held her.

"Muffy must be fed twice a day," said Jeanne. "I will pay you to make two visits each day, morning and evening."

"I'm sorry, but I go to work at 5:00," Ginny broke in.

Jeanne looked shocked. "Very well," she said. You can stop by on your way to work. Now, in the morning Muffy eats the wet food. In the evening, give her the dry food. If you give her dry food in the morning, she'll choke. And make sure she has fresh water in her water bowl at all times."

"Of course," said Ginny softly.

"Muffy and I take two walks every day," Jeanne went on. "We walk down to the end of the street and back again. Her leash is hanging in the hall closet. Don't forget to put on her jacket. We wouldn't want her to get a chill, would we?"

Right then, Muffy jumped out of Jeanne's arms.

"Here, girl!" Ginny called to the dog. She wanted to see if Muffy would come to her. She wanted Muffy to get to know her before Jeanne went away.

Muffy came right over. Ginny picked her up and patted the fur on her little head. Muffy acted like Eva's dog. But Eva's dog didn't wear a jacket.

"I can't believe she took to you so fast," said Jeanne. "I guess she won't miss me so much after all." For a moment, Jeanne looked a little sad. But then she perked up. "Very well. That's why I'm hiring a pet sitter, isn't it?"

"How can I reach you while you're away?" Ginny asked. She set Muffy back down on the floor.

"I'm visiting my sister in France," Jeanne said. "But you have my main number. You can text me anytime. And here is my email address. I would like a report on Muffy every day."

"Thank you," Ginny said. "And I'll need a key or code to get into the house."

"Oh, of course," said Jeanne. She picked a key up off the hall table and handed it to Ginny.

"Is there anything else I can do?" asked Ginny.

"I stopped the mail," said Jeanne. "But would you be so kind as to water my plants on Saturday?"

"Sure," said Ginny.

"One more thing," said Jeanne Hobbs. She reached for a little bottle. "Muffy needs her drops every morning. Two drops on the tongue. She's very good about taking her drops."

All of this was a lot for Ginny to remember. Wet food in the morning. Dry food on the second trip. Keep the water bowl full. A walk to the end of the street twice a day. Don't forget the jacket. Water the plants. Two drops on Muffy's tongue every morning.

As soon as Ginny got home, she wrote it all down. Then she got a bright idea. She typed up and printed a client information form for people to fill in. Using the form, she would never forget to ask all the important questions. She would always know what to do and when.

And then she went online to pay for the liability insurance and bonding.

Ginny could see that pet sitting was a real business. She didn't want to make any mistakes.

4

Troubles with Muffy

Ginny's visits with Muffy went fine for the first three days. She took the little dog for walks and always put the tiny red jacket on her. "You look pretty silly to me," Ginny told Muffy. "But you're supposed to wear your jacket when you go out, so that is what you'll do." It was Ginny who felt silly walking down the street with Muffy in her red jacket.

Ginny followed all of the other directions, too. She gave Muffy two drops on the tongue every morning. She watered the plants. She did everything on the list and she did everything right.

But on the fourth morning, Ginny forgot to bring her list of tasks. Somehow, she couldn't remember which kind of food to give Muffy.

"Is it wet food or dry food in the morning?" she asked Muffy. The dog looked at her and gave a cute little bark. So Ginny gave her the dry food. Sure enough, Muffy began to choke. She was having trouble getting air. She couldn't even bark. She pawed at her face.

Ginny's dog Rocky had never choked. She didn't know what to do. She would have to call the pet doctor.

"Oh, no!" Ginny said out loud. "I forgot to ask for the name of Muffy's vet!"

Then Ginny remembered how Jeanne Hobbs had found her number. Ginny had visited only one vet's office, so that's the one she called.

The woman on the phone asked Ginny how big Muffy was. "She's small," said Ginny. The woman told Ginny to pick up Muffy by the back legs and turn her upside down. Then to shake her a bit.

The trick worked. Muffy began to breathe again.

Then the woman at the vet's office sent a video called *How to Help a Choking Dog* to her phone. Ginny gave Muffy some wet food and watched the video while the little dog ate. The video showed how to push on a dog's chest to clear the throat. Ginny watched the video over and over. She wanted to be ready if she ever needed to help a choking dog again.

Ginny would be sure to add another question to her form: "Veterinarian to call in case of emergency?"

Jeanne wasn't angry when Ginny told her about the choking. "Thank you for saving my Muffy's life!" was all Jeanne said.

Each day after that went much better. On Saturday, Ginny watered the plants. There were no problems for the rest of that week. And then, Ginny went to the house to feed and walk Muffy for the last time.

Getting ready to leave, she remembered that she had forgotten to ask what to do with the key on her last day. She took it out of her pocket. She started to lay it on the kitchen table. Then she stopped herself.

What if Jeanne doesn't get home today after all? Ginny decided to hold on to the key, just in case.

On Monday morning she went to Jeanne's house to return the key. She rang the bell, even though she had the key. No answer. Then Ginny heard Muffy. The little dog was crying on the other side of the door.

Ginny used the key to open the door. No one was home except poor Muffy. The little dog was hungry. Ginny knew that Muffy needed her drops. She went inside to take care of her.

Why hadn't Jeanne Hobbs called? Ginny wondered what could have happened.

Later in the day, Ginny returned for the second visit. This time, Jeanne was there—and she was very upset. But she wasn't angry with Ginny.

"I'm so glad you kept the key!" said Jeanne. "I can't believe my message didn't go through! My plane was late. It would have been terrible if you couldn't get into the house this morning. Thank you for thinking to check on my baby."

"I was happy to," said Ginny.

"In fact, dear, I'd like you to keep the key," said Jeanne. "I'm sure I'll use your services again. And besides, it will be good to know that you have it.

Jeanne Hobbs paid Ginny for a full extra day. She gave her a nice tip, too.

Ginny went home and added another line to the client information form: "Please call or text as soon as you get home. And make sure I get your message." She had to be sure a pet would never be left alone for long.

Everything had gone fine with Eva's dog. But Ginny wasn't happy with the Muffy job. Too many things had gone wrong. She had made mistakes.

"Every business runs into problems," Eva told Ginny. "You worked things out. You learned some lessons. Sometimes you just have to learn from your mistakes."

Ginny laughed. "Isn't that the truth."

"So when are you going to quit your crummy job?" Eva asked her.

"That's a long way off," said Ginny. "But it's something to work for."

5

All Kinds of Animals

Ginny's next adventure starred a parrot named Pete. It was her first bird-sitting job.

Pete's family said that he was really a person. He only *looked* like a bird. He even talked. The family had taught him to say smart-sounding things like "Hello!" and "Up here!" and "Pretty bird!"

Sometimes Pete came out with strange sounds of his own. Maybe his owners were right. Maybe he really *was* a person with feathers. Anyway, Ginny thought that Pete was very funny.

One day when Ginny went to see Pete the parrot, he was gone! The door to his cage hung open. The cage was empty. And the house was quiet.

Oh, no, Ginny thought. *They told me how much that bird cost. Plus, they think he's a person. If he got away, they would never speak to me again!*

She began to search the house. She looked upstairs and downstairs. She looked in every closet. She looked high. She looked low. She even looked in the back yard.

No Pete.

Ginny sat down on the sofa and cried. Then she thought she heard a noise. She stopped crying to listen. But she didn't hear anything. The sound must have been her own crying.

"I never should have taken on a bird," she said out loud.

Then she heard the noise again. This time when she stopped to listen, she heard the words, "Up here!"

It had to be Pete. It just *had* to be. But where was his voice coming from?

"Up here!" Ginny heard again.

She tried to follow the sound. It led her up the steps to the second floor.

"Pretty bird!" No question about it. This was Pete talking.

The noise led Ginny into the bathroom. It was the one room she had not searched. There was Pete, sitting on top of the shower door.

"Hello!" he chirped.

"I do not believe this!" Ginny said. She put out her hand. Pete jumped on. She carried the bird back to his cage.

"You don't like being in a cage all the time, do you?" Ginny said. "Well, I'm sorry. You're a *bird*. I don't care what they say. You look like a bird. You sound like a bird. You eat like a bird. A very smart bird, for sure. But you *are* a bird. So don't forget it, OK?"

"Pretty bird!" Pete said.

Ginny laughed. She was so glad the parrot was all right.

When Pete's owners got home, Ginny told them what had happened.

"Oh, he does that all the time," they said. "He knows how to open his cage. We should have told you."

That day Ginny added yet another item to the client information form: "Does your pet have any unusual habits I should know about?" How nice it would have been to know about Pete's little habit right from the start.

Then there was Pipper the cat. Pipper would not eat unless his dish was placed straight in line with the door. His owners had written this on the form. But Ginny didn't believe it until she saw it for herself.

As a test, she turned Pipper's dish sideways. She knew that the cat was hungry. But he walked away from the dish and left the room. A few minutes later, he came back in. The dish was still sideways. Pipper pushed the dish with a paw but he couldn't get it straight.

Finally Ginny put the dish straight in line with the door. Pipper ate as if he hadn't eaten in days.

When he finished eating, Ginny picked him up and gave him a hug. She sat down on the sofa with the cat on her lap. He purred and purred as she stroked his fur.

"You miss your friends, don't you?" she asked Pipper. He let out a meow. Ginny was sure that he was answering her question.

Then Pipper fell asleep. Ginny lifted him off her lap and set him down. It was time to leave, and she still had to clean the litter box. She had saved her least favorite job for last.

Ginny's favorite job of all was walking dogs. She liked to walk anyway—and she just liked being with dogs. *I can't believe I'm getting paid for this*, she would think to herself.

She got to know many different kinds of animals. One time she took care of a pair of rabbits. Another job was for two turtles and a hamster. Once she even pet sat a snake! She had never liked snakes. But pretty soon, her fear of snakes was gone. She even learned to wear the snake around her neck!

For just a few days Ginny took care of a horse. She had to brush the huge animal from head to tail. She fed it sugar cubes out of her hand.

But when the call came to take care of a pet pig, Ginny drew the line. She had heard that pigs made good pets. But she didn't want to find out for herself. "I'm sorry," Ginny told the caller. "I don't pet sit for pigs." There was just something about pigs she didn't like. She was a pet sitter, not a farmer!

Every business has its limits.

6

A Growing Business

Ginny's whole plan seemed to be coming together. She kept a calendar of dates and times. Now she always knew where she was going and when. And every day was different. She liked that.

She put a tag on every house key and kept door codes in her phone. She marked each tag or code with a client number, not an address. No one but Ginny would know which number went with which address.

At each home, Ginny fed the pet or pets first. Then, while they ate, she watered plants or cleaned up messes. After that it was TLC time. Dogs got a walk. Cats got her lap.

Before she left each home, Ginny wrote a little report for the owner. Then she went around the house and turned lights off and on. From the outside, it always looked as if someone was at home.

Back in the car, Ginny wrote down the number of miles she had driven. She kept these records to report on her taxes.

In the beginning, she went back to each house to get paid. Then she started sending bills online. Most people paid online, or they could send a check.

And, of course, Ginny kept track of all the money coming in and going out.

Even though every job was different, one thing was always the same. The animals were always happy to see Ginny. They knew that if Ginny was there, they had a friend. And they knew she would be back again soon.

Word spread about Ginny's pet-sitting service. She was getting lots of work. She was on the move most of every day. Then she went on to her job. Some days she hardly got a break at all. Business seemed almost too good. Ginny was getting very tired.

In November, the calls came like rain. People were getting ready to go away for the holidays.

Ginny's thoughts were a jumble. She didn't know what to do. She already had more work than she could handle. She even turned away some business. She was tired and couldn't think straight.

That's when her friend Eva said, "Don't you see? It's time to quit your job!"

Ginny broke out in a big smile. She knew Eva might be right. But quitting a job is a big thing to do. She would have no more paid sick days. No vacation days. No steady paycheck. She would have to buy some health insurance.

Before Ginny did anything crazy, she had to study some numbers.

She looked over her records. She checked to see just how much money she was making. She added up how much she needed to live.

Then she looked at how much she might make if she didn't turn away work. With the holidays coming up, she could be very busy. But what about after that? No question, certain months would be slow.

"Big deal!" said Eva. "What's the worst thing that can happen? You find another crummy job!"

Ginny wished she could be as carefree as Eva. But in her heart she knew that Eva was right. Everyone has only 24 hours in a day.

"That's it! I'm going to quit my job!" she said.

That night she gave her boss two weeks' notice. Starting the next day, Ginny stopped turning down pet work. Instead, she took every job that came her way. She was pleased with herself. She felt lighter than air.

She loved to get up in the morning, throw on old clothes, and go out to visit animals. Pets didn't care what she looked like.

But her problems were not over.

7

Holiday Blues

The holidays were very, very busy for Ginny. She was running around like a crazy person. She was forgetting to do some of the tasks listed on the client information forms. She was forgetting to write up everything she did in the reports at each home. She forgot to cut Brandy the poodle's nails.

When Brandy's family got home they called Ginny right away. They had more to say than, "We're home now."

"You forgot to cut Brandy's nails!" cried an angry voice on the phone.

"I did?" Ginny said. "I'm so sorry."

"You'd *better* be sorry!" the woman said.

"Gee, do a few days without cutting Brandy's nails really matter?" Ginny asked.

"When Brandy's nails get long, they scratch our wood floors," said the woman. "A poodle's nails are very sharp!"

"I see. Well, I'm really sorry." Ginny thought her client was making a big deal out of what happened. But her pet-sitting service was a business. In business, the customer is always right, even if they're not right. "Did Brandy's nails scratch your floors?"

"Well, no," said the woman. "But that was just lucky."

"I'll be more careful next time," Ginny promised.

"There won't *be* a next time!" And the woman hung up the phone.

Ginny didn't say anything. She didn't need a client like this. *You win some, you lose some*, Ginny said to herself.

A few days later there was a problem at another home. As she opened the door she saw that everything inside was dark. How could that have happened? She thought she had left two lights on yesterday. She must have forgotten.

Ginny carefully stepped inside and turned on the hall light. When she looked into the living room, she couldn't believe her eyes. Two lamps lay broken on the floor. A flower vase lay in pieces with water all around. The place was a mess. The dog had turned over everything in sight. He had even chewed on the chair legs.

Just then, the dog crawled out from behind the sofa. He held his head down. He knew he had done something very wrong.

Ginny had a few words with the dog. "Bad boy!" she told him. "Look what you've done!" Then she patted him on the head. Her voice turned soft. "You were lonely, weren't you?" she said to him.

She cleaned up the mess and wrote in her report what had happened. Then she called the insurance company.

She hoped she would never have to make a claim, but that is what insurance is for.

How in the world am I going to get through the holidays? Ginny asked herself. Hanukkah was early that year, followed by Christmas and New Year's. The whole month of December was booked solid. There would be no let-up in business all through the month. And the phone calls kept coming.

So she called Eva.

"You said you wanted a part-time job, right?" Ginny asked her friend.

Eva was happy to help out. She would be a contractor, not an employee. Ginny would pay her for each visit she made. She took Eva along on a few jobs, then gave her client information forms and keys to use on her own.

The day before Christmas brought snow. Hour after hour, it snowed and snowed. By Christmas morning everything was covered in a thick, white blanket. Ginny looked out the window. Her car was buried deep in the snow. Her heart sank. "Now what will I do?" she wondered.

That day she was glad she was still living at home with her mother and brothers. The family had three snow shovels. Ginny and the boys got to work. They cleared her car and the driveway in less than an hour. An hour later, the snowplow came through. Ginny backed her car into the street.

Then Ginny thought of Eva. Eva's car was terrible in snow. Even if she could dig it out, it would be dangerous to drive. Ginny called her friend.

Nothing worried Eva. "No problem," she told Ginny. "The bus is running. I'll just put on my boots and take the bus. I'll get as close as I can to my stops and then walk."

"You're great!" Ginny said. "But listen. We'll be lucky to make it to every place *one* time. Don't even think about making any second trips. Just give the animals extra food and water. And don't walk any dogs. Just take them outside to do their business and come back in. Got it?"

"Got it," said Eva.

It was hard to believe, but Ginny made all of her visits that day. Eva made all of hers. At some places, they had to make their way through a foot of snow just to get to the door. If there was no porch, they had to clear snow just to open the door.

But they made it. They *had* to. Those pets were just too important.

Long after dark, Ginny got home. She was tired and hungry. Her mom heated up what was left of the Christmas dinner she had made earlier. Ginny enjoyed every bite of it, even if she had to eat alone.

There was still snow on the ground after Christmas, but no new snow. It became easier and easier for Ginny and Eva to make all of their visits. But they were still very busy up to New Year's Day.

Ginny missed having down time over the holidays. She missed watching sports on TV with her brothers. Ginny thought about it. She saw that giving up some fun was part of running her pet-sitting business. It was a price she was willing to pay.

8

Time to Sell

Ginny's business was a whole different story after the holidays. Some people took winter vacations. But most stayed home during the cold weather. It was true that Ginny needed a break. And she had expected business to slow down. But she never expected things to be *this* slow.

It was time to put out the word again.

Ginny set up a Facebook business page and an Instagram account. She was glad she had taken pictures of the pets she looked after along the way. Now she had lots of sweet faces to post. She started following other accounts in hopes that they would follow her back. She put free ads on internet listings.

She also went back to the pet store and to more veterinarians' offices. She wanted to make sure that everyone knew she was still around. And she left them with more of her business cards.

Most people were booking their trips online these days. But she went to a travel office that was still busy with group travel.

"Let's make a deal," said Ginny. "I'll write your business name on the back of my cards. You give out my cards. If a customer of yours books my pet service, I will give you 10% of what I charge them."

Sure enough, Ginny got a few jobs through the travel office. It was worth paying a little to get that winter work.

Then she thought some more about who else would need a pet sitter. She thought of working people. Don't their pets get lonely while they're at work? Maybe they would pay for someone to look in on their pets during the day, or walk their dogs.

So Ginny went around to all kinds of businesses. She gave out her card at offices all over town. Sure enough, she got more work, mostly walking dogs.

One day, Jeanne Hobbs called. Ginny had taken care of Muffy three different times. She thought Jeanne was calling to ask her again. But instead she told Ginny that Muffy had died.

"She choked on her dry food," Jeanne explained. "And in the evening! Can you believe that, my dear? You took better care of her than I did! I should have known what to do. Now my heart is broken."

Ginny knew how much Muffy had meant to Jeanne. Good thing she had bought a box of cards just for pet owners. She sent Jeanne Hobbs a card and wrote, "Muffy was my first real pet-sitting job. I'll never forget her."

Not long after that, Jeanne bought a puppy. She called Ginny and said, "That card meant so much to me, dear. I'd like you to come by and meet my new Buffy. I got a little boy this time!"

Ginny took Buffy a gift of chew sticks to cut his teeth on. Jeanne Hobbs was very pleased. Ginny sent the card and brought the gift out of kindness. But she also knew it made good sense to keep her clients happy.

Then one day Ginny got a call from a pet shampoo company. The man asked if she might want to sell good pet shampoo. She could also sell brushes and combs for cats and dogs.

"You can make a lot of extra money with our products," said the man. "Everything we make is so good it will sell itself!"

"I haven't sold products before. Do I have to buy anything up front?" Ginny asked.

"Not a thing," the man promised. "We give you a starter kit with shampoo samples and product lists. Plus a few of our brushes and combs. All you do is show them to your customers. Let them try the samples. Then take their orders and send them to us. The products will be delivered to the customers' homes."

"Sounds like I can't lose," said Ginny.

"There's no way you can lose," said the man. "With our pet products, everybody wins. You, me, and most of all the pets!"

So Ginny began selling the pet shampoo, brushes, and combs. She made a dollar here and a dollar there. The dollars added up.

Ginny made one more business move during the slow months. She gave her pet-sitting service a name. She believed a real business name might add something.

She thought up many names. She checked to see what names were already in use. Pet Keeper, Critter Sitter, Animal Watcher, Home Pet Care—all of those were taken.

Ginny thought and thought about what makes a good name for a pet-sitting business. For one thing, the name should be easy to remember. For another, it should be different, but not too different. Most of all, it should put into words what was really special about her service.

Then Ginny came up with just the right name. She checked and no one was using it. From now on her business would be known as Tender Loving Pet Care, or TLPC. Ginny registered the name, and, by law, she placed a notice in the newspaper.

Now she had to get new business cards. It was a good thing they didn't cost much to print online. The new card said TLPC in big letters across the top. Under that were the words Tender Loving Pet Care. On the side was a paw print. And at the bottom were her name, number, and email address.

Ginny sat back in her chair and looked out the kitchen window. She saw patches of green grass poking up through the melting snow. Spring was on its way!

Winter had been a good time to look ahead. New ads. New contacts. A new name. A new business card. New products to sell. Ginny the pet sitter was ready for anything. Nothing could slow her down now.

9

Pet Taxi

Ginny's best shampoo customer was Jeanne Hobbs. "Buffy won't let me wash him with anything else," she said. So Ginny made many trips to Jeanne's house just to drop off a bottle or two. She wondered how often Buffy got a bath, because Jeanne was buying a lot of shampoo.

One day when Ginny was delivering shampoo, she found Jeanne with a cast on her leg. "What happened to you?" Ginny asked.

"I fell down three little steps," said Jeanne. "I won't be able to walk for months. Can you believe it, all this trouble over three little steps?"

"That's too bad," said Ginny. "Is there anything I can do to help?"

"Yes, my dear, there is," said Jeanne. "You can take Buffy on his walks. And he's supposed to go to the vet tomorrow. It's time for his next shots. Do you think you could drive him there? Heaven knows, I can't!"

Ginny said she could do that. But she didn't have a pet cage. She didn't want a little dog loose in her car. Good thing Jeanne had a cage.

So the next day Ginny came to get the little dog. She loaded Buffy into the cage and off they went to the vet's.

Buffy did not know what to make of the ride. He had never been in a car with anyone but Jeanne Hobbs. Ginny was very glad he was in a cage. She couldn't believe that a little dog could make such a big mess as Buffy made in that cage.

Ginny stayed with Buffy while he got his shots. She held him still and patted his head as the needles went in. She knew that was what Jeanne would have done if she had been there.

When they got home, Jeanne paid Ginny well. That gave Ginny the idea to offer a pet taxi service. She could take animals anywhere they needed to go. Usually that meant going to the vet or the groomer.

She bought pet cages in three sizes. She worked out the cost per mile and hour. Then she posted on Facebook: PET TAXI SERVICE. RIGHT ON TIME. LOW RATES. Calls started coming in. She also set up a calendar online. The time blocks starting filling up.

It was great to find more work for slow times. She knew the busy times would come again. She could always turn down pet taxi jobs if she didn't have time. Or maybe Eva could help out.

Then a call came out of the blue. It was from Pipper's owner. Ginny remembered Pipper. He was the cat who would eat only with the dish in line with the door.

"I heard about your pet taxi service," said the woman. "You know that Pipper eats a special kind of cat food. But the only place to buy it is 20 miles away. Could you pick up Pipper's food once a month?"

Ginny said she could do that. She wouldn't have to do it at a certain time of day. When she had an extra hour, she could fill it with a drive to the store.

Before long, she was picking up special food at the same store for three customers. All of them were older people. She was getting paid three times for one drive! The pet store gave her a special deal.

Still, it was a lot of running around. Sometimes it was hard to find the time to not only pick up the food but also deliver it. She wondered if there might be a better way to do the deliveries.

Ginny was getting used to thinking up new ideas. A new idea for the pet food came fast. She started ordering the food online. It would be delivered straight to each person's home. Ginny did all the work on her phone. No more running around.

Ginny told her clients that they could do the online ordering themselves. They didn't have to hire her to do it.

But some people weren't used to using computers. They were happy to pay her for the service.

Late one night Ginny was getting ready for bed. She didn't expect the phone to ring at that hour. It sounded louder than usual.

"This is Jeanne Hobbs, my dear," came the voice. "Something awful has happened to my Buffy! He can hardly move and he won't eat. I think he got into some poison. I called the emergency vet. The vet told me what to give Buffy, but I don't have it. Can you drive us to the vet's office right away? The doctor said she will be waiting for us."

"I'll be there in a flash," said Ginny.

Buffy lay still in the cage in the back seat of Ginny's car beside Jeanne. From the front seat, Ginny couldn't hear him breathing. But she heard Jeanne talking to him all the way to the emergency vet's office. "Hang on, little guy!" Jeanne said. "We're almost there. You're going to be all right!"

Ginny ran through five red lights. The streets were empty at that hour. Her brakes screamed as she pulled into the vet's parking lot.

"We're here, Buffy!" Jeanne cried. "Hang on! Hang on!"

Ginny picked up the cage and burst into the vet's office. The doctor was waiting. She pushed a pill into Buffy's mouth. She rubbed the dog's throat to help him swallow. "Good boy," she said. When the pill was down, Buffy licked his own nose. But his eyes were still closed.

"Now let's hope it works," the doctor said to Jeanne and Ginny.

They waited for what seemed like hours. Really, it was only a few minutes. Then, slowly, Buffy opened his eyes. Ginny could hear him breathing again. Jeanne took one of Buffy's paws and rubbed it between her hands. Then Buffy threw up on the table.

"Looks like he's out of the woods," the doctor said. "He's going to be fine. That was a close call."

10

Animal Friends

"You are so lucky, I can't stand it," Eva was saying to Ginny. "You have your own business. Do you know how great that is? You don't have to worry about being laid off. And you don't have to put up with a boss. I call that lucky!"

"It's not just luck," said Ginny. "I built this business, and I work hard. I put up with a lot! And remember, I don't get a paycheck every week or two. When I don't work, I don't get paid. True, I don't have one boss. I have lots of bosses—my clients!"

"Yes, yes," said Eva. "But still, you're lucky. Things might not have worked out. You might be working at some crummy job again. Why, you even save lives! Rocky would have been proud of you."

Ginny still got tears in her eyes when she thought of Rocky. "All right, I'm lucky," she said. "So why don't you start your own business?"

"Well, I've been thinking about it," Eva said. "You know how I like to groom Poppy? I think maybe I'd like to be a dog groomer."

"Why not?" said Ginny. "Except you would have to clean out other dogs' ears, too. I know how you hate that."

"I could learn to live with it," said Eva. "I mean, can't you just see me as a dog groomer? What fun! I could clip, clip, clip all day long. Poodles and spaniels and mutts and whatever! But no pit bulls. I simply will not touch a pit bull."

Ginny laughed. "And you can put that nice perfume on the dogs when they're done."

"And a bow around the neck!" Eva added.

"Oh, yes," said Ginny. "Don't forget the bow."

"There's a dog-grooming training program," Eva said. "Three months, part time, that's all! I have signed up for the course and plan to become a licensed dog groomer. Isn't that great? Can you stand it?"

So that's what Eva did. She kept her day job while she went to school. When she was finished she set up a shop in her basement. It wasn't easy. She had to file forms to get a business license. And she had to get a bank loan to get all the grooming tools she would need.

Eva's shop had everything. The main item was the grooming table. Eva also had to buy good clippers, cages, and hair dryers. Right next to the floor drain was a big tub with a hose. If any water spilled out when she was giving dogs a bath, it wouldn't be a problem.

Eva loved to wear a bright pink shirt when she worked. The dogs knew her by her pink shirt.

Eva turned out to be really good at animal grooming. Ginny told her she was "cut out for it." She told Eva to show her work to the vets. They had sent Ginny many new clients. Maybe they would send customers to Eva, too.

So Eva gave her own dog, Poppy, a first-class grooming. That dog looked like a princess and smelled like a rose. Eva put a bow around Poppy's neck and drove her to the vet's office a few blocks away.

"Well, isn't she the prettiest girl in town!" said the lady at the front desk.

Eva left some business cards. Within a few days, she was getting calls.

Ginny told her customers about Eva's grooming business. Eva told her customers about Ginny's pet-sitting service. Just like always, the two friends were a big help to each other.

Ginny Carr's business kept growing and doing well. About a year later she bought a used van. That worked much better than her car.

Soon after that, Ginny moved into her own place. That's when she decided she was ready for a new dog. She had always wanted a black Lab. Maybe now was the time.

She drove her van over to the animal shelter. She looked at all the dogs in the cages. She looked at their eyes most of all. One by one, she looked for eyes that melted her heart.

And then it happened. The dog was still a puppy, but a big puppy. It was black, but not a pure Lab, just a cute mutt. Girl or boy? It didn't matter. This dog was the one. This was the one with the eyes that melted Ginny's heart.

The puppy turned out to be a boy. Ginny named him Rover, a common old dog name she always thought was funny. Like Rocky, Rover grew very large. Like Rocky, Rover always had a baby face. Ginny loved him. And just like Rocky, Rover loved Ginny back—no matter what.

Made in the USA
Las Vegas, NV
23 March 2021

20055329R00030